QUIZZES FOR MARRIED COUPLES

FUN RELATIONSHIP QUESTIONS AND QUIZZES
FOR COUPLES TO TAKE TOGETHER

MR. & MRS. L

© Copyright 2020 - All rights reserved Admore Publishing

Paperback ISBN: 978-3-96772-033-4

Hardcover ISBN: 978-3-96772-034-1

The content contained within this book may not be reproduced, duplicated or transmitted without direct written permission from the author or the publisher.

Under no circumstances will any blame or legal responsibility be held against the publisher, or author, for any damages, reparation, or monetary loss due to the information contained within this book. Either directly or indirectly.

Cover Design by Rihan W. Cover artwork from DepositPhotos

Published by Admore Publishing: Roßbachstraße, Berlin, Germany

www.publishing.admore-marketing.com

CONTENTS

Getting started — v

OUR RELATIONSHIP
1. Our Relationship — 3

LIKES & DISLIKES
2. Likes & Dislikes — 11

FIRSTS & LASTS
3. Firsts & Lasts — 21

HOBBIES & INTERESTS
4. Hobbies & Interests — 31

BEST QUALITIES
5. Best Qualities — 41

FOOD & DRINKS
6. Food & Drinks — 51

ENTERTAINMENT
7. Entertainment — 61

FAMILY & FRIENDS
8. Family & Friends — 71

PETS & ANIMALS
9. Pets & Animals — 81

TRAVELING
10. Traveling — 93

MONEY
11. Money — 103

PHYSICAL APPEARANCE & CHARACTER
12. Physical Appearance & Character   113

INTIMACY
13. Intimacy   123

THE PAST
14. The Past   133

THE FUTURE
15. The Future   143

BUCKET LIST
16. Bucket List   153

Afterword   161
Thank You   163

GETTING STARTED

"My wife and I were happy for 20 years - then we met."
- Rodney Dangerfield

Have you ever felt this way about your significant other? Like you have been together for years, but you still don't really know each other? Or, maybe you are newly married and still learning about the secret habits of your new spouse. Whether you have been together for decades or only for a few months, there is always something new to learn about your partner.

But how can you go about learning new things about someone you are already married to? Aren't you suppose to know everything about your spouse before you get married?

No way!

People are complicated creatures, and relationships themselves are complicated as well. However, we know that it can be a challenge to reconnect and rediscover someone after marriage. Our quizzes are designed to be a fun and interactive way to keep your marriage growing and developing long after the I-do's.

Why Take Our Quizzes

Discovering new little facts about your spouse is a fantastic way to reconnect and help your marriage grow stronger. That is why we have put together this fun and informative quiz book for married couples. You will find tons of quick quizzes that you and your spouse can do together within these pages. They will help you find out more about each other, your relationship, and your marriage in general.

Maybe you will take a quiz and find out that your spouse secretly drinks the milk out of the carton or that they don't remember your grandmother's first name. Maybe you'll take a quiz and discover that you both don't like your mother's lasagna. Or perhaps you take a quiz and learn that the best part of your spouse's day is waking up to your smile. Good or bad, funny or annoying- you are definitely going to go deep into your relationship to find out new things!

What Will You Learn About Your Spouse

Wondering what you will learn about your spouse through our quizzes? You will learn, well, almost everything! We have made a wide array of quizzes to help cover many facets of your relationship and yourself. There are quizzes about your likes and dislikes, things that interest you, and even quizzes about how you feel about your spouse (but how you _really_ feel!). We have tried to ask deep, personal questions as well as lighter, more amusing questions. The main goal is to keep your relationship open and the thrill of discovery part of your marriage. We promise that you will learn a lot about your spouse (*who is that person next to you in bed anyway?! Time to find out!*).

A Game Changer, Not a Life Changer

This quiz book is designed to be a fun activity for you and your spouse to do together. We want to help strengthen your bond in an entertaining way. However, this quiz book is not meant to fix your relationship if you have marital issues. If this is the case, we strongly suggest assessing your marriage and talking to your partner on a more serious level. Always put happiness and health as a top priority for you and your spouse, and remember that communication is key. But, if you and the love of your life are just looking to push your relationship forward in a new, creative way, then it's time to start taking some quizzes!

On that note, we bet that you are ready to dive into our first quiz. Are you ready to learn your spouse's favorite ice cream flavor? Are you ready to find out what they love most about you? Are you ready to hear all about their top pet peeves? Then cozy up on the couch with your partner and get ready to start asking some questions- *it's quiz time*!

OUR RELATIONSHIP

1

OUR RELATIONSHIP

"My most brilliant achievement was my ability to be able to persuade my wife to marry me."
- Winston Churchill

So you got married. Congratulations! Now, let's assess your relationship... In this chapter, we will find out a lot about you and your partner's roles in your relationship and how the two of you became a perfect match. This section will also show how you perceive each other within your marriage. Do you feel like you are pulling all the weight in the marriage? Or do you feel like you and your partner are equals? We will find out in a fun (and fast) way! Being equals in a relationship is essential, and taking this quiz can help you achieve that perfect balance of love and responsibility.

To take this quiz, you will need to work fast- no time to think! Read one of the questions and then immediately say your answer. You can also choose to write down your answers, so you and your partner can take the quiz simultaneously. Respond as quickly as possible on paper and then go over the answers after the quiz is over. By writing down your answer rapidly, you will be going with your gut instinct for each answer, which can be very telling! For example, if you write down your own name to answer the question "Who makes the best coffee?" you better be prepared to make the coffee every morning from now on! If you write down your partner's name for the question "Who fell in love first?" you might have some explaining to do!

Are you ready for your first quiz? This relationship quiz will set the tone for the rest of our quiz book and maybe for the future of your relationship. Answer honestly and answer quickly! Ready? Set. Go!

Directions

Read the questions out loud and answer with your name or your partner's name. Answer each question as quickly as possible to ensure that your answers are honest. You can choose to write down your answers and share the results with each other after the quiz is complete or simply answer out loud immediately after the question is read.

OUR RELATIONSHIP

Who is more likely to leave dishes in the sink?

Who makes the best coffee?

Who is more *"responsible"*?

Who has the healthiest diet?

Who is the best driver?

Who is more likely to lose their keys?

Who fell in love first?

Who is more daring?

Who is the messiest?

Who is the hardest worker?

Who is more romantic?

Who is the best gift-giver?

Who is more likely to get lost?

Who is more likely to be running late?

Who is smarter?

When you first met, who made the first move?

Who is more likely to wake up grumpy?

Who is the better dresser?

Who is better at keeping secrets?

Who is the better athlete?

LIKES & DISLIKES

2

LIKES & DISLIKES

"You'd be surprised how much you can have in common with someone completely different from you"
– Anonymous

Are you feisty while your partner is overly calm? Are you a fan of the beach while your partner would rather be skiing in the mountains? They say that opposites attract and that two different personalities can make a marriage balance. Liking different things can actually be great for your relationship! As long as you know what makes each other happy, you will have a successful relationship. When you manage to make your differences complement each other, the result is magical!

But what exactly does your partner like? Do you know? And do they know what you like and dislike? It's time to find out! You may learn that your partner actually prefers things that are very different from you or, that you are actually more inline than you previously thought!

This quiz is a great learning tool and, while you may know most of the answers, some might surprise you!

Instructions

Ask your spouse each question and have them either record the answers on a piece of paper or simply answer aloud. Take some time to talk about each answer, elaborating on why you like or dislike certain things. If you think of other questions along the way, be sure to ask!

LIKES & DISLIKES

What is your partner's favorite color?

What is your lover's favorite TV show?

If your partner could meet one famous person, who would it be?

What is your better half's favorite season?

What if your partner's favorite thing about you?

Would your love rather spend a night:

   a.   *Out on the town*   *b.*   *Cuddled up at home*

Who is your partner's favorite family member?

What is your partner's favorite sport to play and their favorite sport to watch?

If your partner could live anywhere in the world, where would they live?

What is your better half's favorite food?

What one thing can your partner not live without?

What is your significant other's biggest pet peeve?

What one activity does your partner hate doing?

Does your partner prefer:

a. Cats
b. Dogs
c. Birds
d. Reptiles
e. No animals

Would your partner rather:

a. Wake up early
b. Sleep in late

True or False- Your spouse loves kids.

<u>True</u> / <u>False</u>

Would your partner rather have:

a. An apartment in a city
b. A condo on the beach
c. A mansion in the mountains
d. A house in a regular, rural town

What is the best thing that your lover does for you?

What about your relationship makes you really happy?

True or False- your spouse likes to cook.
True / *False*

FIRSTS & LASTS

3

FIRSTS & LASTS

"My wife Mary and I have been married for 47 years and not once have we had an argument serious enough to consider divorce; murder, yes, but divorce, never"
– Jack Benny

There are many firsts and lasts in a marriage. From your first dance to your first kiss as a married couple, a marriage does not mean the end of new things within your relationship. Sure... some things come to an end (you'll never have to go on a first blind date again!), but all happy beginnings come from other endings. So let's talk about some of those firsts and lasts within your relationship so far.

Who was the first to say I love you? And what was your first impression of your significant other? Thinking about how your relationship began can be fun. You may even remember some fun times that you had forgotten. Maybe all the "firsts" weren't good, like your first fight. But, you learned how to work through it, and relationships can grow through hardships. You shouldn't ignore the trickier "firsts" in your relationship!

Now let's talk about those "lasts" that come with every marriage. The last time you are considered single. The last time you go on a first date. The last time you are the only person with access to your bank account. The last time you have to sleep alone.

Lasts may seem final, but they can also be good. You may really appreciate that marriage means you will never have to go on a first date again! Who likes all that stress and anticipation anyway?!?

Throughout your marriage, there will be many firsts and lasts, and the only sure thing is that your spouse will be there with you through all of them. This quiz will take a look at all the firsts and lasts that have already happened and see if you can remember them clearly. We hope that thinking about all of these times will get you excited for what the future of your marriage will look like.

Instructions:

Many of the questions in this quiz will require longer answers, so it is best to ask your spouse the question and then have them say the answer aloud. Take time to talk about each question and relive some fun (and maybe some not so fun) times you had in your relationship.

FIRSTS & LASTS

When did you first meet your partner?

What was your first impression of your partner?

a. You were immediately attracted to them

b. You did not like them

c. You wanted to just be friends

d. Other

What was the last awesome meal that your partner made?

What did you and your partner do on your first date?

When did you first know that you were in love?

What was the last nice thing your partner did for you?

When was the last time that you slept alone?

Who was the first person in your partner's family that you met?

a. Mom
b. Dad
c. Sibling(s)
d. Other

When did you first consider marrying your lover?

Who was the last person you dated before your partner, and why did it end?

Where did you go on your last date?

Where did you and your better half go on your last vacation?

When was the first time your partner annoyed you?

True or False- You remember what your wedding song was.
True / _False_

What was the first movie you watched with your partner?

Where was the first place you and your partner lived together?

What was the last time your lover made you laugh?

What was the name of your partner's first pet?

Who started your first fight?
a. You *b.* Your partner
c. Both of us

If you have kids, would you rather have:
a. Boys *b.* Girls
c. Both *c.* Neither

HOBBIES & INTERESTS

4

HOBBIES & INTERESTS

"90 percent of marriage is just shouting "what?" from the other rooms".

- Anonymous

Did you and your spouse bond over a love for sports? Or maybe you met at a comic book conference. Many couples first fall in love over a common interest or hobby; however, it is almost impossible that you and your spouse like *all* of the same things. Everyone has their own personal preferences and pastimes, and there is a good chance that some of them vary from what you like. But, let's find out!

The goal of this quiz is to see if you know the things that interest your partner. It may also help you learn about some new things they like. You may even find that you both have a hidden interest in something, giving you a whole new pastime to bond over! You may also find that something your partner once loved may have faded into the background. After all, hobbies can change over time, and something that your spouse used to love may have changed. A sky diving obsession may quickly fade with age, or the love of running may end after years of bad knees! However, a love of cooking may have sprouted, or an interest in gardening could be growing. This quiz will reveal all of those things!

Directions

This quiz has multiple choice questions and also open-ended questions for you and your partner. Feel free to write down your answers and then discuss them afterward, or simply answer aloud as you go through the quiz. If none of the multiple-choice answers seem fitting, feel free to elaborate and make your own answer- there is no right or wrong here!

HOBBIES & INTERESTS

What is one thing you cannot live without?

Would your partner rather:

- *a.* Read a book
- *b.* Listen to music
- *c.* Go for a run
- *c.* Watch TV

What is your lover's favorite pastime activity?

What activity has your partner always wanted to try?

What is your favorite thing to do with your partner?

What meal does your partner like the best:
- *a.* Breakfast
- *b.* Lunch
- *c.* Dinner
- *c.* Dessert

What is one unique thing that your partner specializes in?

What is one hobby that both you and your partner share?

What new activity or hobby would you like to
try as a couple?

What is one thing that interests you that you do not think
your significant other would like?

What was your partner's favorite past time as a child?

If you could be an expert in any field, what would it be?

What is one hobby, activity, or interest that you think your partner would be good at?

Which one of these things does your partner need to have?

- a. Your pets
- b. Homemade food
- c. Their garden
- d. Their car
- e. The TV
- f. Other

Which of these is the most important to your better half:

- a. Career
- b. Education
- c. Marriage
- d. Sleep
- e. Music
- f. Friends

Which of the following TV channels is your partner most likely to watch:

- a. News Channel
- b. Comedy Central
- c. Food Network
- d. HGTV
- e. Sports Center
- f. Disney Channel
- g. Netflix
- h. No TV

What kind of books does your partner like to read?

- a. Mystery
- b. Romance
- c. Fantasy
- d. Non-Fiction
- e. Biography
- f. Other

Who is more likely to turn on the TV, you or your partner?

Name one hobby that both you and your better half share.

Between the two of you, who is more likely to try new things and who is more likely to stick to their favorite hobbies and activities forever?

BEST QUALITIES

5
BEST QUALITIES

"I love you not only for what you are, but for what I am when I am with you".
– Roy Croft

There is probably a lot that you love about your significant other- you did choose to marry that person after all! But what do you love the most? What qualities does your partner possess that made you love them? Everyone is attracted to different things. Whether it be your partner's smile, laugh, or caring personality, the things you are drawn to are important to celebrate. People who openly talk about why they fell in love and what they love about their partner are more likely to have long-lasting relationships. We all know that communication is key, and you should be sure to communicate and praise what you love about your spouse.

In this section, we will take a look at your best qualities and what your partner believes to be your best qualities. This is a great quiz to take when you both need a little encouragement and positivity. Maybe you just had a bad day at work, or perhaps you and your spouse fought over who's turn it was to do the dishes. If you're feeling a little grumpy, take this quiz with your partner, and you will be sure to feel good by the end of it. Thinking about your positive traits always feels good! You may also discover some new things about yourself that you never knew were so loveable. Did your partner ever tell you how much they love the sound of your voice? Or how they like falling asleep to your cute, soft snore. No one knows you better than your partner, and it's time to find out exactly why they love you.

Directions

This quiz has multiple choice questions and also open-ended questions for you and your spouse. For this section, we think it's best to answer each question as they are asked and elaborate on each answer aloud. Talking positively and openly is essential to a marriage's success, and this quiz will help you open up and express your feelings in a fun and upbeat way. Remember to focus on the positives- this quiz is all about the best things regarding your partner!

BEST QUALITIES

What was the first physical trait that you noticed and loved about your partner?

Which word best fits your spouse:
- a. Caring
- b. Selfless
- c. Supportive
- d. Daring
- e. Exciting
- f. Timeless
- g. Other

What specific personality trait attracts you the most to your partner?

What is one good deed or action that your significant other did that you will never forget?

In what way do you wish you could be more
like your spouse?

What quality do you hope your children inherit
from your partner?

If you had to pick just one, which of the following is your
significant other's strongest trait:

- *a.* Hard-working
- *b.* Sweet
- *c.* Beautiful
- *d.* Smart
- *e.* Other

What physical characteristic does your
better half possess that you love?

What trait does your partner have that others are
always talking about?

What is your partner's greatest success in life thus far?

If your spouse was walking down the street and saw someone fall, what would they do first:

- *a.* Call 911
- *b.* Rush over to help
- *c.* Walk in the other direction
- *d.* Call for others to help
- *e.* Other

What kind of animal does your partner remind you of, and why?

What one thing do you think makes your significant other special and sets them apart from everyone else?

What is something that your partner does within your marriage that you appreciate?

What do you find inspiring about your love?

What personality trait do you think your spouse loves about you?

What do you consider to be your own personal best quality that people love and admire?

Name something that your partner is passionate about.

Which person in the relationship is the optimist?

Which person in your relationship is the better communicator, and who is the better listener?

FOOD & DRINKS

6

FOOD & DRINKS

"A woman's place is in the kitchen…..sitting with her feet up, sipping a cocktail and watching her husband cook dinner."
- *Anonymous*

From first dates to everyday life, food and drinks play a major role in every relationship. There is a good chance you and your spouse first got together to eat and drink...

Most relationships begin this way! Now that you are married, you likely eat together multiple times a day. Meals are a central part of a marriage, and they can be a time to bond. Sometimes they can also be a source of small arguments (aka asking your partner over and over again "what's for dinner?"!). Food has power!

This quiz will show the role that food plays in your relationship and see how it can help you make your marriage even stronger. We will also see how much you know about your partner and their eating habits. Did you know that your spouse drinks 6 cups of coffee a day?

Or that they hate that lemon salmon you make? Now is the time to get all those food preferences out there while taking a fun quiz- maybe it will help you avoid those food arguments later on! Be sure to be honest and straightforward- you never know what may be revealed in these quizzes (maybe your spouse hates *making* that lemon salmon too!).

Did you know that many studies have actually been done regarding food preferences and personality traits? People who like sweet foods have been said to be more agreeable, while salty food preferences have been linked to competitive personality traits. If you enjoy spicy food, you may be considered a risk-taker! Does your partner like sour foods? Then they may be described as someone who has high standards. It is fascinating that what we eat can not only nourish us and bring us together, but also show who we really are!

Directions

This quiz will give you an insight into how important food and drinks are in your relationship and unveil your spouse's true food preferences. Make sure that everyone is in a good mood as you may learn that your spouse hates eating something you love. If it's easier, write down your answers so you can express your feelings clearly. Of course, you can also always answer aloud. Read each question and take turns answering each question fully before moving on to the next question.

FOOD & DRINKS

What is your partner's favorite dinner?

Which of these would your spouse prefer for breakfast:
- *a.* Pancakes or waffles
- *b.* Cereal and milk
- *c.* Eggs and bacon
- *d.* Yogurt
- *e.* A smoothie
- *f.* Skip breakfast

What was the first meal you and your lover had together?

What is your partner's favorite restaurant?

What kind of cuisine is your partner's favorite:

- a. Italian
- b. Mexican
- c. Chinese
- d. Indian
- e. BBQ
- f. Other

What is your significant other's signature dish to prepare?

What is your favorite food that your partner makes?

Who is the better chef- you or your partner?

Would you consider your spouse to be an adventurous eater?

Does your significant other follow a specific diet plan, and, if so, what diet do they follow?

Does your partner have any food allergies?

What is your spouse's favorite alcoholic drink?

How does your love prefer their coffee:

- a. Black
- b. Cream and sugar
- c. Coffee creamer
- d. Just milk
- e. Just sugar
- f. No coffee
- g. Other

What is your partner's favorite dessert?

When eating at a restaurant, what is one menu item that your significant other is sure to order?

Which fast-food restaurant would your spouse choose:

- a. McDonald's
- b. Taco Bell
- c. Panera Bread
- d. Chipotle
- e. Dominos
- f. Chic Fil A
- g. Other

Would your spouse rather go out to dinner with a group of friends or alone with you?

What is your significant other's favorite pizza topping?

True or False- your partner would rather go out to eat instead of cook at home.

True / *False*

If your partner had to only eat one snack food for the rest of their life, what snack would they choose?

ENTERTAINMENT

7
ENTERTAINMENT

"A divorce lawyer is way more expensive than a babysitter- make date night a priority!"

- Anonymous

What should we do tonight? This is probably a very common question in every marriage. The things you choose to do together as a couple or alone can play a significant role in your relationship. Maybe you love to go out dancing while your partner would rather stay at home. Or maybe you both love playing video games together and seeing who can get the highest score. From concerts to sports games, dinner and drinks, to Netflix at home, you have to stay entertained somehow!

In this chapter, we will ask lots of questions about your entertainment preferences and see how your personality shines through in relation to your choices. Would you rather stay in and read a book, or are you the kind of person who waits in line for hours to buy tickets to that new blockbuster movie? And are your favorite pastimes the same as your spouses, or are they vastly different? While everyone may have different entertainment preferences, most couples have some common hobbies that they can bond over. Having things that you like to do together is just as important as having things you enjoy doing alone.

Are you ready to take a fun quiz and find out more about your partner, yourself, and you as a couple? Entertainment related questions can reveal a lot! You may even discover something new that you both like, giving you new date ideas for the future. The dinner and a movie date set up never gets old!

Directions

For this quiz, you and your partner are going to write down the answers to each question. If you have ever seen the show "The Newlywed Game", that is precisely how you will play! Read each question out loud and write down your answer and also how you think your spouse would answer the same question. For example, if the question was, "What is your partner's favorite movie?". You would write down what you think your partner's favorite movie is and write down your own favorite movie. Once the quiz is complete, you and your partner will read the answers and see how well you really know each other's favorite entertainment choices!

ENTERTAINMENT

What is your partner's favorite movie?

What is your lover's favorite book?

Would your partner rather:
- a. Go to the movies
- b. Read a book
- c. Play a video game
- d. Watch a TV show
- e. Go to a ballet
- f. Go for a hike
- g. Other

What was the first movie you and your spouse saw together?

What is your partner's favorite type of music?

- *a.* Country
- *b.* Classic rock
- *c.* Pop
- *d.* Rap
- *e.* Electronica
- *f.* Jazz
- *g.* Blues
- *h.* Musical theater
- *i.* Other

What is your spouse's favorite TV show?

Has your better half ever seen a live play, and, if so, what was it?

What movie has your significant other been wanting to see?

What is your spouses favorite kind of entertainment date:

- a. Dinner and a movie
- b. Going to an arcade
- c. An outdoor adventure
- d. A day with other couples
- e. Going to a club to dance

If your partner was to plan the perfect date night, what would it involve?

True or false: Your spouse loves to cuddle up on the couch
and watch a movie with you?

True / *False*

Would you describe your taste in TV to be the same
as your better halves?

Yes / *No*

Who is your partner's favorite actor or actress?

If your significant other was a cartoon character,
who would they be?

Does your partner like watching sports? And, if so,
what is their favorite sport to watch?

Could your spouse live for one week without a TV?

<u>Yes</u> / <u>No</u>

Does your partner like watching reality shows?
If yes, what is their favorite reality show to watch?

Do you consider your spouse to be good at video games?

<u>Yes</u> / <u>No</u>

What genre of books does your partner prefer:

- *a.* Romance novels
- *b.* Fairy Tales
- *c.* Non-Fiction
- *d.* Historical
- *e.* Biographies
- *f.* Dramas
- *g.* Mysteries
- *h.* Poems

If your significant other was on a deserted island, what kind of entertainment would they absolutely need?

FAMILY & FRIENDS

8

FAMILY & FRIENDS

"The difference between in-laws and outlaws? Outlaws are wanted"
- Anonymous

When you get married, you are essentially marrying an entire family. After you say "I Do", you are instantly part of a whole new family, and with that comes a new dynamic. You may love some of your new family members just as much as you love your spouse. However, there may be some people in your "new family" that you could do without! Of course, the same goes for your spouse as they become an official member of your family. As much as you may like to think that it is just you and your partner in your own little world, this couldn't be further from the truth. Many people are involved in your relationship, from family to friends!

Couples come into a relationship with their own set of friends as well as their own family. Merging these two worlds can be challenging, but also fun. You may meet some amazing people through your spouse and build new relationships that last a lifetime. However, on the other hand, there may be that one friend of your significant other that you just can't stand. Navigating these relationships is essential to your success as a couple. Talking about your feelings regarding various people in your lives is vital to your marriage. You shouldn't keep it a secret that you don't like your husband's Aunt Sally dropping by anytime she'd like! And you should tell your wife that you love spending time with her dad. It is not just you and your spouse in a relationship but also all of your family and friends as well.

This quiz is designed to get you talking about the people in your lives and reveal some true feelings that may have been held back. Honesty is always the best policy in a marriage. Now it's time to talk about all the people who are also "involved" in your marriage in one way or the other. Get ready!

Directions

Talking about how you feel about certain people in your life is essential. So, for this quiz, read each question aloud and then discuss your answers rather than writing them down. While some answers may be quick and require no discussion (everyone agrees that Uncle Matt is the funniest guy in the family!), you and our spouse may disagree on other answers. Each question is worth talking about as interpersonal relationships can build and break a marriage. Let's work on making yours stronger through honesty and openness! Time to answer some questions!

FAMILY & FRIENDS

Who is your favorite person in your spouse's family?

Out of all your partner's friends,
who do you get along with most?

If there was one person in your significant other's family
that you would rather never see again, who would it be?

What is your favorite thing about your partner's mother?
And their father?

Which of your love's friends do you butt heads with the most?

Name all of your partner's friends that you also consider to be your personal friends.

Has someone in your significant other's family ever told you a secret? If so, what was it?

What are your spouse's grandparent's full names?

Where did your partner meet their best friend?

Do you remember the first time you met your significant other's family? Where were you, and what happened?

How often does your lover talk to their best friend?

Does your family like/love your partner, and why?

Did your family and friends approve of your marriage?

Would you feel comfortable around your spouse's family without your spouse around?

Do you feel like you are part of your partner's family, or do you feel like they exclude you?

Were you and your significant other friends first? Or was there instant attraction?

Would your spouse rather have dinner with:

- a. Group of friends
- b. their entire family
- c. Just you
- d. Eat alone

What is your partner's favorite thing to do with their friends?

Write down the names of all your spouse's immediate family members (siblings, aunts, uncles, grandparents, and cousins).

You never have to see one of your partner's friends ever again- who is it?

PETS & ANIMALS

9

PETS & ANIMALS

"It's tough to stay married. My wife kisses the dog on the lips yet she won't drink from my glass."
–Rodney Dangerfield

Are you a pet lover? Is your spouse allergic to dogs? Do you still have a pet from a different relationship? Pets and animals play a big part in a marriage as they are just as present in your life as your partner! The way you and your significant other feel about pets and animals can help you bond as a couple and pull you apart. Having a pet together can also reveal new characteristics of your spouse. Maybe you didn't know your partner was such a cuddler until you saw them cuddling the dog all day! Animals can be such a fun and exciting part of a relationship, and, in this chapter, we will explore just that.

There are many ways in which a pet can change your relationship with your partner. If you get a pet together, you will have less free time as that pet will need attention and care. However, a pet may help you and your spouse be more active and responsible. You may also feel jealousy toward your pet if your spouse seems more interested in the animals than you. However, having a pet together can also make you a family. So, let us find out how you and your spouse feel about pets and animals. Maybe you both have been secretly wanting a dog! Or maybe, you both agree that you never want pets in your house. Animal relationships can be just as telling as human relationships!

Directions

Many of the questions in this section will show how much you know about your spouse's history with animals. Other questions may lead to long conversations about future pets in your household. Rather than write down your answers, just answer each question in this section out loud. Read the question and then give both you and your spouse a chance to answer.

PETS & ANIMALS

What was your partner's first pet, and what was the pet's name?

Is your significant other:

   a.   A cat person   *b.*   A dog person

   c.   A reptile person   *d.*   A no-pet person

What is your spouse's favorite kind of animal?

Did your partner have a favorite pet when they were growing up?

If you and your significant other had a dog, who would walk it more?

What would your partner say if you brought home a pet snake?

True or false: Pets bring you closer together as a couple.

True / _False_

In a perfect world, how many pets would your partner have?

If you were in the wild and saw a bear, what would your significant other do?

- *a.* Run away
- *b.* Take a picture
- *c.* Scream
- *d.* Hide in a tree
- *e.* Help you
- *f.* Other... (elaborate)

True or false: Pets bring you closer together as a couple.

True / *False*

In a perfect world, how many pets would your partner have?

If you and your partner got a dog, what would you feed it?

- *a.* Regular dog food
- *b.* Organic dog food
- *c.* Table scraps
- *d.* A raw meat diet
- *e.* Let it hunt for itself.

Who is the bigger animal lover, you, or your spouse?

If your partner was an animal, what would they be?

Who is more likely to volunteer at your local animal shelter?

Who wants pets more- you, your partner, or both of you want pets equally?

Is your partner allergic to any kind of animal?

How many pets would your lover consider too many?

If you and your spouse adopted a cat today,
what would you name it?

If you could have any exotic animal in the world as a pet,
what would it be?

What kind of animal adventure would your partner prefer:

- a. Safari in Africa
- b. Arctic animal expedition
- c. Trip to the zoo
- d. Big snake encounter
- e. A trip to the local animal shelter

Does your significant other prefer to be around people or animals?

TRAVELING

10

TRAVELING

"In life, it's not where you go but who you travel with"
– *Charles Schulz*

Seeing the world as a couple can be very different from traveling alone. It is exhilarating to visit new places, and when you have the chance to do it with someone you love, it is even better. Of course, not everyone loves to travel. Some people would far rather stay home and enjoy life in the area they know and love. Other people can't get enough adventures. Are you and your spouse on the same page when it comes to traveling?

Traveling together can also reveal new things about your partner as you step out of your comfort zone and into the big, open world. How does your partner react when the airport loses their luggage? And what is the first thing your partner says when they see the Grand Canyon? You may find that you are married to someone who appreciates the vast beauty of new places, or you may find that your spouse would much rather curl up on the couch and stay put. This quiz will help you talk about your travel goals as a couple and see where your marriage will take you.

Directions

This is a fun quiz to write down your answers for each question and then go over the answers at the end. You can compare your answers to your spouses and see if you both feel the same about traveling or if you have different preferences. Think about each answer on your own, and don't let your spouse see what you write!

TRAVELING

Where is one place in the world that you would love to visit?

Where was the first place you and your partner traveled together?

Do you prefer to travel by:

a. Train   *b.* Plane
c. Car   *d.* Boat

What was the best vacation you ever took, and why?

Would you rather travel with:

a. Family   b. Your partner
c. Alone   d. A group of friends

Name 5 countries you would love to visit.

Does your significant other have a valid passport?

When traveling, would your partner rather stay in a resort, motel, private house, or tent?

What was the first vacation you ever went on as a kid?

What would your dream vacation be?

Do you prefer to travel to new countries or visit places in your own country?

Would you ever go on a surprise vacation? Or do you need to know where you are going before you leave?

How many places have you and your love visited together?

What are some things that you require on a vacation? A beach? Seclusion? A local bar? Make a list!

Where in the world would you never want to travel?

If you and your significant other could live in any country in the world, where would you both want to move?

Does your partner have any fears about traveling?

Who would you consider more adventurous, you or your partner?

When going on a trip, who packs the lightest? Who brings too much?

What is one thing you feel is necessary to bring on any vacation?

MONEY

11

MONEY

"Money may not buy love, but fighting about it will bankrupt your relationship."
– Michelle Singletary

Whether we like it or not, money plays a huge role in every relationship. It doesn't matter if you are a millionaire or just struggling to get by. Everyone has money issues, which can affect your marriage. Money management is a team effort. It is essential that you and your partner are on the same page when it comes to spending money and also making money! Once you are married, you should make sure that you agree about how the money you both make is shared. Do you both just keep your own income and spend it as you'd like? Do you pool your money in one bank account and have joint access? Does one of you support the other monetarily? These are all important things to work out to ensure that money does not get in the way of your happiness!

It can be tricky to talk to anyone about money-related matters. Still, you need to be able to talk to your partner about any monetary issues. You should also both have a full grasp of your overall financial situation. If you are in debt (which many of us are!), you and your partner should make a plan to pay off that debt together. If you have a little extra cash coming in, decide how you both want to spend it, as a couple! This section will help you start talking about money through fun and informative questions. Money is a part of life, so it's time to break the ice and start the conversation!

Directions

As we mentioned before, it is crucial that you and your significant other can talk freely about money. With that in mind, ask each question out loud and then pause to answer and discuss. Have both you and your partner answer thoroughly before moving on to the next question. Some questions will be quick to answer, while others may lead you into deeper dialogue!

MONEY

Who manages your household finances?

Which one of you is a better saver?

Who in the relationship is a better bargain shopper?

If your partner suddenly had a million dollars, what would be the first thing that they buy?

Your significant other got a bonus in their paycheck, what do they do with the extra money?

- a. Save it
- b. Splurge on a big purchase
- c. Give it to you
- d. Spend it on a night out
- e. Hide it
- f. Donate it

Which one of you has a better credit score?

Who values money more, you or your partner?

Do you feel that you and your partner are equals in terms of income, spending, and money management?

Do you consider your spouse to be financially successful?

Does your partner have any debt? And if so, how much?

What is the biggest purchase your love has ever made?

Is there something that your spouse is currently saving money for?

Would you give your partner unlimited access to your bank account? Why or why not?

True or false- you and your spouse share a credit card.

<u>True</u> / <u>False</u>

Do you find people with money more attractive?

How do you define success?

What do you think your significant other spends most of their money on?

What is the maximum amount you think your partner can spend before consulting you?

What does your spouse spend money on that makes them happy?

Write down 5 financial goals that you have and then talk about each one.

PHYSICAL APPEARANCE & CHARACTER

12

PHYSICAL APPEARANCE & CHARACTER

"Do you believe in love at first sight? Or should I walk by again?"
- *Anonymous*

Were you instantly attracted to your partner? Or maybe you had hundreds of conversations before you first laid eyes on each other. No matter if you knew your partner before or saw them for the first time, physical attraction plays a large part in a relationship. It is almost essential that you have some kind of physical connection with your spouse for your marriage to be successful. What attracts one person to another can be very specific. Some people may feel a connection to a person who has a great smile, while others may be looking for a particular body type. What attracts you to someone else is as unique as you!

So what was it about your spouse that first caught your eye? And what physical features and characteristics have fueled your relationship ever since? In this chapter, you will find out! As you go through this quiz with your partner, keep the mood light and fun. We all have physical insecurities, and the goal of this chapter is to make you feel good about your body and yourself. Remember that your partner loves you and all of your flaws! No one is perfect, and this becomes more and more apparent throughout years of marriage. So let's get back to those fun, little attractions that you and your significant other had in the early days of your relationship and talk about the bigger things that attract you to one another now.

Directions

Grab a pen and some paper and have you and your spouse write down the answers to each question in this quiz. Once you have answered all the questions, take turns reading them out loud. Don't be afraid to elaborate on your answers or ask your own questions when you hear your partner's answers. This quiz is meant to be fun and exciting, revealing what physical attractions drive your relationship. Have fun, you beautiful love birds!

PHYSICAL APPEARANCE & CHARACTER

What was the first physical feature that you noticed about your spouse when you first met?

What is one great physical trait that your partner possesses that people talk about? (Does she have nice hair? Does he have a winning smile? Etc.)

True or false, you were instantly physically attracted to your significant other.

True / *False*

What is your partner's favorite feature of themselves?

- a. Eyes
- b. Hair
- c. Body
- d. Butt
- e. Chest
- f. Height
- g. Smile
- h. Abs
- i. Other

What physical trait does your lover possess that makes you swoon?

Who takes longer to get ready to go out, you or your partner?

Who owns more beauty products? You or your partner?

Do you think that a good wardrobe can make a person more attractive?

What physical characteristic makes your significant other stand out in a crowd?

What is one physical trait that your spouse is self-conscious of?

What personality trait do you find most attractive about your partner?

If offered a job as a model, would your spouse take it?

Name something that your partner has done that made you more attracted to them.

When you daydream about your love, what are you thinking about?

Do you consider your significant other to be:

Low maintenance / _High maintenance_

Who takes longer showers, you, or your partner?

Who in the relationship is more likely to spend a lot of money on maintaining their appearance?

True or false, your partner could go one week without looking in a mirror.

True / *False*

Do you have a favorite photograph of you as a couple? What makes it your favorite?

If your spouse drastically changed their hair, what would your reaction be?

INTIMACY

13

INTIMACY

"Love is a fire. But whether it is going to warm you heart or burn down your house, you can never tell."
– Joan Crawford

Marriage is the most intimate relationship that you will ever have. Every marriage should have both physical and emotional intimacy that grows and develops over time, creating an amazing bond between you and your spouse. But what drives that intimacy? And how can you make that bond go even deeper? Taking this quiz is an excellent place to start!

The word intimate is defined as something private and personal. Before marriage, you likely had your own life, your own secrets, and lots of privacy. Once married, lots of this changes. Living with someone and being their partner in life means that intimacy shifts, and two people are now involved. Of course, this is a great thing! Having someone to share your life with is what marriage is all about. Many of us crave that intimacy, and that is why we pursue relationships and marriage. Now that you have it, it is time to think about what intimacy is to you as a couple. This quiz will ask you many questions about intimacy and make sure you and your partner are on the same page.

Directions

Intimacy means being extremely close. The only way to get closer to your spouse is to open up, tell the truth, and have long discussions about, well, everything! This quiz is designed to ask you and your spouse questions that may lead to longer conversations. Try not to give quick, one-word answers but really dive into each answer fully. The more you talk, the more intimate you will become! Ask each question out loud and then have both you and your spouse respond.

INTIMACY

When you and your partner first started dating, who made the first move?

Do you consider your sex life to be:

   a. Amazing   *b.* Pretty good

   c. Alright   *d.* Average

   e. Needs improvement

You and your spouse likely lead busy lives. In a perfect world, how often would you want to be intimate with your partner?

Who do you think puts more work into your relationship and keeping it exciting? You or our significant other?

What is your biggest fantasy?

Do you have any secrets that you keep from your partner?

Who is more likely to make the first move, you or your spouse?

What always puts you in the mood for romance?

- a. Music
- b. Alcohol
- c. Dancing
- d. Payday
- e. A fun night out
- f. Just seeing your spouse
- g. Other

The biggest obstacle in your sex life is:

- a. It's a low priority
- b. Limited privacy at home
- c. Don't feel connected
- d. Tired at the end of the day
- e. Other

True or false- you feel comfortable talking about intimacy with your partner?

True / *False*

Who is more adventurous in the bedroom, you, or your significant other?

What would you define as the most intimate part of your relationship?

What do you like the best about your sex life?

What do you dream about most often?

When you think about going home to your significant other, what is the first thing that pops into your mind?

Is there a part of your intimate relationship that you feel needs work?

Name one thing that you think would bring you and your lover closer together.

Do you think that having kids would/did change your intimacy levels?

Do you believe that marriage made your sex life better?

Is there a specific time that you and your partner were intimate that you think about frequently? When was it, and why do you think you remember it so well?

THE PAST

14

THE PAST

"When one door closes, sometimes you want to get a hammer and nails to make sure it stays shut"
- Anonymous

Some may say that you should never look back, leave the past in the past. Others may say that you should always look back, there is a lot to learn from the past. No matter how you feel about the past, it can definitely shape your future! This is especially true in relationships as things that happened at the beginning of your marriage can help you build a stronger relationship going forward. Your personal past may also play a significant role in your marriage, and exploring that can be necessary. No matter how much you would like to forget things that happened in the past, it is essential to confront them. At the other end of the spectrum, celebrate the fun things you experienced!

In this quiz, you will answer all kinds of questions about your past and your spouse's past. It is time to celebrate, relive, and learn from the past! After all, it brought you and your significant other together and put you where you are today. Most of the questions in this section will help you and your spouse remember things that happened long ago, and get you talking about all the good times you had. Other questions may bring up historical events that you learned from and hopefully have moved on from. At the end of the quiz, you may both agree to keep some of the events in the past and never bring them up again! But hey, you live, and you learn. Now you will be able to move forward as a couple.

Directions

This quiz should be more like a conversation. Read each question and then have both you and your partner answer the questions out loud. Feel free to ask more questions on your own (anything you think of) and take time to really discuss each question fully. You may learn a lot about your significant other based on their past and your past as a couple.

THE PAST

What is your first childhood memory?

What is one thing from your past that you regret?

Who was your first kiss, and when did it happen?

What is one fight that you and your partner had that you still remember to this day? What would help you move on from that fight?

If you could relive one moment from your past, what would it be and why?

If you could change one thing in your past, what would it be?

What is your favorite memory that involves your significant other?

What is your first memory of your partner?

When you think about the beginning of your relationship, would you describe it as:

- a. Exciting
- b. Tumultuous
- c. Friendly
- d. Stressful
- e. Loving
- f. Easy
- g. Other

Where was your first date with your spouse, and would you consider it a success?

When your partner first asked you out or when you first considered asking your spouse on a date, did you have to think about it, or were you immediately interested?

Was your significant other ever in love before they met you?

When did you realize that you loved your partner?

What is one thing you learned from a previous relationship?

What was your most embarrassing childhood moment?

Was your spouse's upbringing:

- a. Strict
- b. Relaxed
- c. Loving
- d. Tough
- e. Other

What is one thing that your partner never got to do in their past that they would like to do now?

What was the best birthday that your significant other ever had?

After your spouse got their license, where was the first place they drove?

What is the biggest thing you have learned about relationships based on your past experiences?

THE FUTURE

15

THE FUTURE

"A successful marriage requires falling in love many times, and always with the same person"
– Mignon McLaughlin

You and your spouse have committed to spending your lives together. So what exactly does the future hold? While no one can predict exactly where you will be in five, ten, or twenty years, you can make some predictions! You and your significant other can also start planning and looking forward to what the future may hold. Isn't it great to have someone by your side for life?!

This quiz will help you, and your spouse think about your future goals and how you want to shape your future. It is essential that you are both on the same page and support each other's ambitions. Now is the time to plan! This is a quiz that you can take again and again, pulling it out every so often to reassess your future as a couple and as an individual. Things can change quickly, so it is always good to rethink your plans.

Maybe you and your partner want to buy a house, and right now, that is your focus. But what about after you achieve that goal? It is great to stay motivated, set new aspirations, and as always, talk to each other about these future plans. Make a note to retake this quiz, maybe even annually. It can potentially be a fun new years eve activity! The future can be whatever you make it.

Directions

After taking all of the quizzes in this book, think about which style worked best for you and your partner. Which style quiz did you enjoy the most? Do you like to write down your answers and read them afterward? Do you enjoy answering each question aloud after it's read and discussing it fully before moving on? Or maybe you like to have one person answer each question in the quiz before having the second person respond. For this quiz, choose your response style based on what worked best for you as a couple. Anything goes!

THE FUTURE

What is your main goal for the future as a couple?

How do you think your partner can best help you reach your future career goals?

As you age, what do you think will be the most challenging for your partner (and how do you plan to help):

- *a.* Losing vision
- *b.* Loss of mobility
- *c.* Memory loss
- *d.* Feeling older than others
- *e.* Death of family members
- *f.* Other

What is one thing you hope your significant other accomplishes in the future?

What do you think will be the most challenging part of your marriage?

How long do you plan on living where you are now?

- a. Forever
- b. 1 year
- c. 5 years
- d. Until your kids are grown up
- e. Leave as soon as possible!

Do you think you will be more in love with your significant other in the future?

How do you plan to keep your marriage exciting in the future, and what would you like your spouse to do to keep things fresh and new?

Do you see your significant other staying at the same workplace?

What role will your spouse's family play in your future life together?

True or False- you would like to renew your vows in the future.

True / _False_

If your partner cheated on you in the future, how would you move forward as a couple?

If your lover had a million dollars to buy a vacation home in the future, where would it be?

What do you envision your lives looking like once you and your significant other retire?

What are your future financial goals as a couple?

Is there something you think your partner wants to happen in the near future? What is it?

How does your spouse plan to care for their aging parents?

In the future, would your lover like to (pick as many as you see fitting):

- a. Live a secluded life
- b. Be surrounded by family & friends
- c. Travel the world
- d. Continue to work indefinitely
- e. Retire early
- f. Have a big family

Who is more of a planner, you, or your spouse?

What one thing will help your marriage flourish in the future?

BUCKET LIST

16

BUCKET LIST

"You can, you should and if you're brave enough to start, you will"
– *Stephen King*

Everyone should have goals. Whether they be personal goals, career goals, or marriage goals, it is essential to strive for something. After all, without a goal, you can't score! So what exactly is on your personal bucket list, and what is on your spouses? Do you both have similar things that you want to achieve in life, or are your ambitions vastly different?

It isn't necessary to have all of the same goals as your partner. In fact, having your own goals can be beneficial and help you grow as a person independent of your marriage. However, it is essential that you and your partner support each other and your respective goals. Being understanding, loving, and encouraging is imperative. It is also great for your marriage and relationship to set goals together as a couple. This is a great way to continue to grow and move forward happily!

This quiz will help you make a list of things that you and your partner want to achieve within your lifetime.

Directions

It is a great idea to write down your answers as you go through this quiz. For this last quiz, you and your partner should answer each question together. Ask the question then discuss your answers. Once you and your partner have decided what the best answer is, write it down. Think of this answer sheet as your commitment to each other and your pledge to work toward checking off these goals. Take this "bucket list" out every so often and assess how much you and your significant other have achieved. Make a new list anytime, adding and crossing off items as you live your lives to the fullest!

BUCKET LIST

Do you and your spouse want to have kids, and if so, how many?

Name one place you want to visit together as a couple.

What is a creative, fun, and different "date night" that you and your significant other want to try?

Do you want to own a house together?

Do you want to have pets, and if so, what kind of pets? How many at once?

What is one major purchase that you and your partner would like to make?

Who is someone that you and your significant other would like to meet together?

Name one person who you would like to have a closer relationship with.

What is the biggest thing you want to accomplish within the next five years?

What is your dream job? And how do you plan on working toward having that dream job?

What is one thing that you want to do daily to improve your marriage?

Do you want to renew your wedding vows?

True or false, you and your partner both want
to go skydiving.

True / *False*

What charity would you like to donate to?

Describe a perfect day with your partner.
When will you make this day happen?

What hobby would you like to take up?

Name one thing that you wish you were really good at.

What is one object that you need to have to be happy?
Do you have it already?

If you were to throw an amazing party,
what would it entail?

Can you make sure to tell your significant other that you
love them, every single day?

AFTERWORD

"A Great marriage doesn't happen because of the love you had in the beginning but how well you continue building love until the end"
- Unknown

After taking all of our fun, informative, and thoughtful quizzes, we hope that you and your spouse learned more about each other now than at the beginning of this book. Communication is key to every relationship, and these quizzes surely got you and your partner talking about all sorts of things! Anytime you are at a loss for conversation, you can always pull out a quiz and retake it- your answers will undoubtedly change over the years.

While this quiz book's main goal was to have fun with your partner, we hope that you also gained some insight into your relationship. There are probably things that you learned about your partner through this book that you never knew. You may have even learned something new about yourself! Be sure to contemplate the answers that your spouse gave and reflect on the conversations you had while taking the quizzes. Hopefully, you and your partner answered everything honestly, and therefore, you should take each answer to heart. The key to your marriage may lie in the answers!

Here is to many more years as a happy, healthy, and fun-loving couple!

THANK YOU

Hi there you beautiful couple!

Thank you for taking these quizzes... We hope you had a great time together and learned some new things about one another.

If you've enjoyed this book, please let us know by leaving an Amazon rating and a brief review! It only takes about 30 seconds, and it helps us compete against big publishing houses. It also helps other readers find our work!

Thank you for your time, and have an awesome day!